STONE AGE to IRON AGE

THE HISTORY DETECTIVE INVESTIGATES

Clare Hibbert

WAYLAND

First published in 2014 by Wayland

Copyright © Wayland 2014

Wayland
338 Euston Road
London NW1 3BH

Wayland Australia
Level 17/207 Kent Street
Sydney, NSW 2000

The History Detective Investigates series:

 Produced for Wayland by
White-Thomson Publishing Ltd
www.wtpub.co.uk
+44 (0)843 208 7460

Editor: Clare Hibbert
Designer: Ian Winton
Consultant: Philip Parker
Proofreader: Lucy Ross

A catalogue record for this title is available from the British Library.

ISBN: 978-0-7502-8177-5

Dewey Number: 936.1'01-dc23

Printed in Malaysia

Wayland is a division of Hachette Children's Books, an Hachette UK company

Picture Acknowledgments: Jane Baker: 14; **Stefan Chabluk:** 13; **Corbis:** 17t (Gianni Dagli Orti), 17b (Skyscan); **Dreamstime:** 5b (Gsmcity), 11b (Chrisp543), 20 (Ian Keirle), 21t (Lowlihjeng), 21b (Thomas Langlands); **Mary Evans Picture Library:** 27; **Shutterstock:** cover t (Matthew Jacques), 5tr (Edouard Coleman), 6c (Creative Nature Media), 8 (Jule_Berlin), 11c (UnaPhoto), 12 (George W Bailey), 22t (Jason Benz Bennee), 25br (marilyn barbone); **Superstock:** 7 (imagebroker.net), 18 (Robert Harding Picture Library); **TopFoto:** 4 (The Granger Collection), 9t (English Heritage/HIP), 9bl (Museum of London/HIP), 19t (Ann Ronan Picture Library/HIP), 26r (CM Dixon/HIP); **University of Cambridge Museum of Archaeology & Anthropology:** 6b (1953.61.A); **Wikimedia:** cover b (Thomas T), folios (QuartierLatin1968), 1 (Michel wal), 2 (Dave from Nottingham), 5tl (Didier Descouens), 10 (RX-Guru), 15t (Dr Peter Hoare), 15b (Andreas Praefcke), 16 (Luis Garcia), 19b (Portable Antiquities Scheme/Victuallers), 22b (CeStu), 23 (Mark Healey), 24t (Bloodofox), 24b (Rosemania), 25bl (Joseph Martin Kronheim), 26l (Nicolas Coustou), 28 (Chmee2), 29t (Thomas T), 29b (Val_McG).

Above: A Stone Age Briton carved this horse on a piece of bone around 12,500 years ago.

Previous page: Made from thin sheets of bronze, this Celtic horned helmet would have been worn for show.

Cover (top): Stonehenge.

Cover (bottom): Ancient prehistoric cave paintings.

CONTENTS

Words in **bold** can be found in the glossary on page 30.

The history detective Sherlock Bones will help you to find clues and collect evidence about the Stone, Bronze and Iron Ages. Wherever you see one of Sherlock's paw-prints, you will find a mystery to solve. The answers are on page 31.

WHO WERE THE FIRST BRITONS?

Early humans reached Britain at least 800,000 years ago. They may have belonged to a species called *Homo erectus*, which had spread across Europe and Asia from Africa. At that time, the British Isles were still connected to mainland Europe.

Today, there is only one kind of human on earth – *Homo sapiens*. But in the early days of human **evolution**, many different species came and went. *Homo erectus* appeared in Africa 1.8 million years ago and was able to make simple stone tools. Historians call the period when early humans were first using stone tools the Old Stone Age, or **Palaeolithic Age**.

Archaeologists have unearthed stone tools used by early humans at **prehistoric** sites in eastern England. These **hunter-gatherers** had crossed the wide land bridge that connected Britain to the continent. They followed herds of animals, from deer to mammoths and woolly rhinos, and killed them for their meat and skins. Early humans may have hunted the larger beasts by driving them off cliffs or into bogs. At night, people made rough shelters or slept in caves. They had fire, but probably couldn't start one. Instead they found smouldering branches after lightning strikes or wildfires and kept them burning.

DETECTIVE WORK

Find out how Ice Age people hunted and lived at a Stone Age site in Derbyshire: www.creswell-crags.org.uk/Explore/virtually-the-ice-age.aspx

This cave painting is 9,000 years old. The first artists painted what mattered to them – the animals they hunted for food.

About 650,000 years ago, Britain's climate turned cold and people retreated to warmer parts of Europe. When the climate heated up again, people returned. There were repeated cycles of **ice ages** and warmer times. New settlers brought new technologies.

Homo heidelbergensis arrived 500,000 years ago with more toolmaking know-how. By controlling how they chipped flakes off **flint**, people could make more sophisticated **hand axes** and specialized tools.

People speared fish with bone harpoons, which they fixed to wooden poles.

The Neanderthals reached Britain 60,000 years ago. They could make fire, and could survive even during ice ages. They buried their dead so they may have had some sort of religion. They disappeared from Britain 40,000 years ago – around the same time as the arrival of modern humans, or *Homo sapiens*. The Neanderthals probably couldn't compete for food as yet another ice age began.

Hand axes like this flint one fitted in the hand. They were used to cut meat, scrape hides clean and dig for roots.

What were harpoons carved from?

Neanderthals were close cousins of modern humans, but they had larger brains and distinctive, jutting foreheads.

In 1921, the English author H.G. Wells imagined a Neanderthal in his short story *The Grisly Folk*:

'Hairy or grisly, with a big face like a mask, great brow ridges and no forehead, clutching an enormous flint, and running like a baboon with his head forward and not, like a man, with his head up, he must have been a fearsome creature…'

WHEN WAS THE MIDDLE STONE AGE?

The period from about 11,500 to 6,000 years ago is known as the Middle Stone Age, or Mesolithic Age. People in Britain still lived as hunter-gatherers, but they led more settled lives. They cleared woodlands and built sturdier shelters, where they would stay for a few months at a time. They had domesticated (tamed) dogs, which enabled them to hunt animals such as deer, elk and wild boar.

Mesolithic people had better tools than their predecessors. They used spear throwers, devices that fired spears farther. They crafted tiny, sharp flint blades called microliths. They made bows and arrows for shooting birds, and nets and baskets for catching fish and shellfish. They made dugout canoes for paddling along rivers and coastlines. For the first part of the Middle Stone Age, a large area of land connected eastern Britain with northern Europe. It disappeared beneath the North Sea by 6000 BCE. Ireland was already separated from the rest of Britain by a strip of sea.

Mesolithic people made timber-framed homes, covered with animal skins or turf for warmth.

Music was an important part of people's lives. They kept time in ritual dances with drums, bullroarers and flutes. At Star Carr in Yorkshire, archaeologists have discovered more than 20 masks or headdresses made from deer skulls. **Shamans** probably wore these during rituals. Perhaps they were trying to connect with the animals they hunted or to enter a trance and come closer to the spirit world.

Mesolithic hunters at Star Carr kept the skulls and antlers of the deer they killed to wear as ceremonial masks.

DETECTIVE WORK

Read about the discovery of Britain's oldest house, built by hunter-gatherers at Star Carr around 8500 BCE: www.telegraph.co.uk/news/uknews/7937240/Oldest-house-in-Britain-discovered-to-be-11500-years-old.html

Mesolithic people may have been cannibals. There are strange cuts in the human skulls and other bones found in Gough's Cave in Cheddar Gorge. Maybe they were victims – sacrifices to keep the gods happy. Another theory is that their brains had been eaten by the living as a mark of respect, thinking it would allow their ancestors' spirits to live on. Some skulls were shaped into cups, which were probably used to hold blood, wine or food in special ceremonies.

These bones belong to Cheddar Man, who lived around 7150 BCE. There are openings in the skull where the brain may have been removed.

Name at least three animals that people hunted in the Middle Stone Age.

In 1997, DNA evidence proved that Adrian Targett, a history teacher in Cheddar, was a direct descendant of Cheddar Man. Visiting Gough's Cave, Targett said:

'I'm glad I don't live down here – it's very dark, dank and dismal. I have been down here before but, of course, I never dreamed that I was standing in my ancestor's home.'

However, archaeology expert Dr Larry Barham of Bristol University believed that life was good for the inhabitants of Gough's Cave:

'There were wild boar, bears and beavers. There were packs of wild wolves, too, but apart from that life was probably pretty good. Cheddar Gorge would have looked similar then and must have been a good spot, with ready-made homes, a spring and forest nearby.'

WHAT DID PEOPLE DO IN THE NEW STONE AGE?

People in Britain took up farming in the New Stone Age, or Neolithic Age. This was the period from around 4000 to 2400 BCE. They cleared trees with flint hand axes and planted crops, bringing seeds from mainland Europe. They also brought over sheep and cows, and tamed native wild boar into pigs.

Farming had begun about 11,500 years ago in Egypt and Mesopotamia (ancient Iraq). Over thousands of years, farming skills spread west through Europe. People learned how to sow, harvest and store crops. By choosing the fattest grains to plant, early farmers slowly changed the wild versions of wheat and barley and achieved better harvests.

Farmers didn't need to move around, tracking animals. They could stay in one place. Neolithic farmers lived in settled villages, building homes of timber and stone. One of the best-preserved New Stone Age villages is Skara Brae in the Bay of Skaill on Orkney Mainland, which was inhabited from about 3200 to 2500 BCE. Its eight houses were built sunk into the ground to protect against the cold. Their roofs had whalebone or timber frames and were covered with moss or turf. Farming produced more food than hunting, so people could have larger families. However, farming was harder work. Women spent most of their waking hours grinding grain to make flour for bread. It was a back-breaking job.

DETECTIVE WORK

Take a tour round Skara Brae: www.bbc.co.uk/scotland/ learning/primary/skarabrae/ content/what/index.shtml

A great storm in 1850 is said to have revealed Skara Brae. However, Orkney historian Ernest Marwick (1915-77) showed that the site was known about decades earlier:

'[In] 1769, James Robertson wrote of the square catacombs [underground rooms] in the Downs of Skaill, and said that in one a skeleton was found with a sword in one hand and a Danish axe in the other.'

Wood was scarce at Skara Brae. The villagers used stone, not only for the walls of their homes, but also for cupboards and other furniture.

Grime's Graves in Norfolk was one of Britain's most productive flint mines. Wooden ladders connected the different levels.

People still made hand axes and other tools from stone and bone, but they became fussier about their materials. In places where there was good-quality flint, people dug mines. These mines were dangerous places. Sometimes one shaft was kept as a shrine, where people could make offerings to the gods. They might have asked to be kept safe or for luck finding good stones. Miners traded their flint for other goods.

Neolithic miners dug shafts using antler picks like this one. They may have farmed red deer to have a ready supply of antlers and meat.

🐾 **What did Grime's Graves' miners wrap the flint nodules in? Can you guess why?**

WHAT WERE STONE AGE TOMBS LIKE?

Once people were living in settled communities, they began to take more care over how they buried their dead. Neolithic people dug underground tombs and then marked burial sites with monuments such as **dolmens**, mounds or **barrows**.

Dolmens consisted of a few huge stone slabs that supported a flat stone, known as the capstone. People erected dolmens all over Europe. The main sites in the British Isles are around the coasts of Ireland, Cornwall and Devon. Not all dolmens have human remains under them. The ones that were not tombs might have been put up as markers to show that a particular family lived on and farmed that area of land.

Mounds could be small or large. One of the grandest is the circular one at Newgrange in County Meath, Ireland. Built about 3200 BCE, it measures 76 m (250 ft) across and has a wall running round the edge. A passage leads to a central chamber, which has smaller chambers leading off it.

J.R.R. Tolkien was inspired by the landscape of Neolithic Britain when he wrote *The Fellowship of the Ring*:

'They heard of the great barrows, and the green mounds, and the stone rings upon the hills and in the hollows among the hills.'

The dolmen at Kilclooney in County Donegal, Ireland, dates to about 3500 BCE. Its massive capstone is the length of a family car.

Newgrange was probably used for special ceremonies. It was designed so that at dawn on the winter **solstice**, a beam of sunlight shone through an opening above the entrance and lit up the main chamber. Other monuments from this time also produced special lighting effects at certain times of the year. To achieve this, Neolithic people must have had some knowledge of astronomy and understood how the position of the Sun in relation to the Earth changed over a year.

Which two shapes decorate the stone at the entrance to Newgrange?

DETECTIVE WORK

Explore the tomb at Newgrange and see what happens there on the shortest day of the year: http://video.nationalgeographic.co.uk/video/places/culture-places/historical/ireland_newgrange/

A beautifully carved stone marks the entrance to the Newgrange mound.

Barrows were simple mounds, covering just one burial chamber. Long barrows, named for their oval or rectangular shape, might cover a group of tombs. The West Kennet Long Barrow in Wiltshire was constructed in about 3600 BCE. It is part of a group of Neolithic monuments that also includes the standing stones at Avebury and Silbury Hill, the tallest human-made mound in Europe. Silbury Hill stands an awe-inspiring 40 m (131 ft) high and would have taken a team of 500 workers about 10 years to build.

No human remains have been found at Silbury Hill. The monument was probably built for religious ceremonies.

WHY WAS STONEHENGE BUILT?

Salisbury Plain's circle of standing stones is Britain's most famous prehistoric site. However, exactly why Stonehenge was erected and how it was used remain a mystery. Over the years, people have suggested that the monument might have been a temple, a burial site, a healing centre or even a kind of calendar.

Stonehenge was built in stages over about a thousand years. The first stage began around 3000 BCE, when Neolithic people dug a circular ditch and bank. This kind of earthwork is called a **henge**. Small pits inside the henge were dug to bury people's ashes after they had been cremated. Some of these pits contain **grave goods**.

There are two types of stone at Stonehenge. The smaller ones, known as bluestones, went up around 2600 BCE. They came from the Preseli Hills in south-west Wales more than 250 km (156 miles) away. They were probably transported using rafts along rivers and rollers on land. They were put up in a double circle but rearranged after the larger stones had been erected. The larger stones, known as sarsen stones, were dragged from the Marlborough Downs using sledges and ropes. Each weighed about 25 tonnes.

The stones at Stonehenge were carefully positioned. At dawn on the summer solstice, the sun rose to the north-east of the circle, between the heel stone and a matching stone that has now gone – the heel stone stands about 77 m (254 ft) from the centre of the circle. At midwinter, the sun set in the south-west, between the gap in the central horseshoe.

This is how Stonehenge would have looked when it was completed.

Bluestone horseshoe

Circle of sarsen stones

Sarsen horseshoe

Circle of bluestones

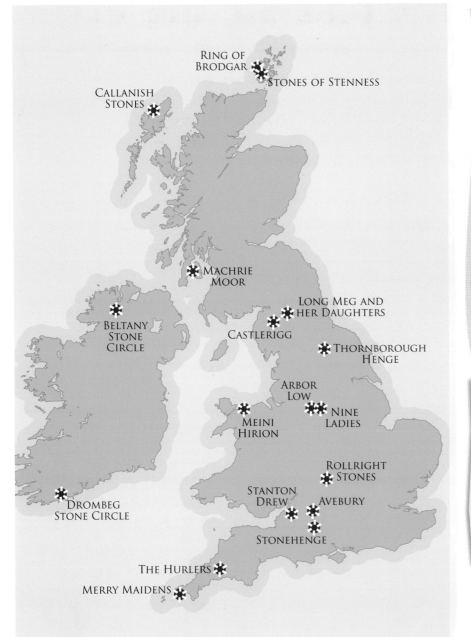

This map shows some of Britain's Neolithic stone circles and henges.

The 12th-century priest and historian Henry of Huntingdon wrote one of the earliest descriptions of Stonehenge:

'*Stanenges, where stones of wonderful size have been erected after the manner of doorways, so that doorway appears to have been raised upon doorway; and no one can [understand] how such great stones have been so raised [up], or why they were built there.*'

DETECTIVE WORK

Explore a clickable map of Stonehenge here: www.english-heritage.org.uk/daysout/properties/stonehenge/world-heritage-site/map/

🐾 **How many sarsen stones made up the central horseshoe shape at Stonehenge?**

Neolithic Britons constructed henges and stone circles elsewhere, too. The Thornborough Henges in North Yorkshire date to between 3500 and 2500 BCE. There are no stones – simply a series of three circular earthworks linked by straight double ditches. Europe's largest stone circle is at Avebury, Wiltshire, just 44 km (27.4 miles) from Stonehenge as the crow flies. Built around 2600 BCE, it is 421 m (1,381 ft) across and contains two separate smaller circles. The Ring of Brodgar in Orkney was put up between 2500 and 2000 BCE. It was originally made up of 60 stones, but fewer than half are still standing.

WHEN DID THE BRONZE AGE BEGIN?

The **Bronze Age** was the period of history when people began to make things out of metal. In Britain, it started around 2500 BCE. The first metal that people learned to work was actually copper, not bronze. Most of the Bronze Age metal objects that survive are copper tools and trinkets.

It is rare for metal to occur in its pure form. Usually it has to be extracted from metal-rich rock, called ore, which is found underground. Techniques for extracting metal were probably brought to Britain by the **Beaker** culture (see pages 16-17). Metalworkers crushed the copper ore using a mortar and pestle. Then they heated it over a fire to melt the metal – a process known as smelting. Finally, they poured the molten metal into moulds. To make copper arrowheads, for example, metalworkers used arrowhead-shaped clay moulds.

After people had learned to shape copper, they began to use tin and gold. By about 2150 BCE, they discovered that copper and tin could be mixed to make a stronger metal, bronze. To feed the demand for bronze, more mines opened up. There were large copper mines at Great Orme in northern Wales and in Ireland at Ross Island, County Kerry and Mount Gabriel, County Cork. There were tin mines in Cornwall and Devon.

DETECTIVE WORK

Find out about the biggest copper mine in Bronze Age Britain: www.greatormemines.info

Today, tourists can explore the tunnels of the Great Orme copper mines in northern Wales.

Metals were used for useful objects, such as tools and containers, and also for display objects. People could show off their high status by wearing fine brooches and bracelets. The most ornate pieces were made of sheet metal that was hammered into shape as it was cooling. The spectacular golden cape discovered at Mold in Wales was made of sheet gold.

These are the two parts of a Bronze Age flesh hook – a tool for pulling hides out of tanning pits or meat out of cooking pots.

🐾 **Which part of the flesh hook has been remade in modern times?**

The Mold cape was made from a golf-ball-sized piece of gold that had been hammered until it was as thin as foil.

The Mold cape was found in hundreds of pieces. Neil MacGregor, director of the British Museum, explained how theories about it changed over time:

'It was thought first of all that it was the breastplate of a pony. Then it was thought to sit over the shoulders of a man, probably a king of some sort. Now we think it was for a woman. It would have sat over her shoulders, stopped her moving her upper arms. She would have been very constrained but clearly it would have been obvious you were very rich and very important.'

WHO WERE THE BEAKER PEOPLE?

The Beaker people are named after the bell-shaped beakers they made, which were decorated with patterns of lines that were pressed into the clay before firing. Their beakers were used to hold mead (a honey drink) and beer, food, metal ore and even human ashes.

The Beaker people appeared in western Europe around 2800 BCE. They were among the first Europeans to work metal. As well as making beakers, they also produced metal tools and arrowheads. They traded the objects they made and their culture spread. Beaker culture and metalworking arrived in Britain about 2500 BCE.

A lot of the information we have about Beaker culture comes from graves. A man known as the Amesbury Archer was buried with five Beaker pots near Stonehenge around 2300 BCE. There were also clothes, tools and weapons. By examining his DNA, scientists discovered that the Amesbury Archer had grown up in the Swiss Alps. Perhaps he was one of the people to bring Beaker culture to Britain?

Beaker culture only flourished in Britain until about 1700 BCE, but trade links with Europe continued. A wooden boat discovered near Dover dates to the 1500s BCE. Archaeologists dug out about 9.5 m (31 ft) of the boat, but the rest had to be left underground. Made of oak planks, it would have been used to ferry tin, bronze and other goods across the English Channel. People also used boats inland. The beautifully preserved remains of eight Bronze Age log boats have been found in an old quarry pit at Must Farm in Cambridgeshire. They would have been used to navigate the watery fens.

Talking about the log boats at Must Farm, archaeology expert Dr Matthew Symonds says:

'I have been lucky enough to visit many excavations over the years, but rarely has the past felt closer than that morning in Must Farm quarry.'

Beaker pots were bell-shaped, and decorated with lines. This one from Spain dates to around 1720 BCE.

🐾 **What clue suggests that the Beaker people believed in an afterlife?**

DETECTIVE WORK

Investigate the Dover boat: www.dovermuseum.co.uk/Bronze-Age-Boat/Bronze-Age-Boat.aspx

Horses were becoming an important means of transport, too. They could pull farm carts and were also useful in warfare, carrying horseback warriors or drawing war chariots. As the Bronze Age continued, there was increasing violence in Britain. Chiefs grew rich and powerful through trade or mining, and fights over territory and resources became common. To protect themselves from raids, people built defensive ditches around their villages.

Discovered in Denmark, this bronze statue is one of the earliest models of a horse-drawn vehicle in Europe. It was made in the 1300s BCE.

This magnificent chalk horse carved into a Berkshire hilltop dates to about 1000 BCE. It is 110 m (374 ft) long.

WHEN DID PEOPLE LEARN TO MAKE IRON?

The first iron objects were made in Britain about 1000 BCE, and by 800 BCE iron had become the main metal being worked. This date marks the start of the **Iron Age**. Iron ore was more common than copper or tin so it was easier to find, but the metal itself was harder to extract. It needed hotter temperatures and, often, repeated heating and hammering.

Within a few hundred years, most tools in Britain were made of iron, and this led to an amazing increase in food production. Using iron axes, farmers could clear greater numbers of trees; with iron shovels and ploughs they could cultivate heavier soils. They were sowing improved varieties of barley and wheat that yielded bigger harvests. Farmers also planted more peas, beans, flax and other crops. Increased food supplies meant better nourished people and an increase in the population. The number of people in Britain went beyond one million.

DETECTIVE WORK

Iron Age people used clay furnaces called bloomeries to smelt iron. Watch an archaeologist give a demonstration: www.youtube.com/watch?v=KP4DjM3jBsw

Iron Age people did not change just the landscape through farming. They also built nearly 3,000 **hill forts** across Britain. These were hilltop settlements, protected by ditches and banks. Some were simple, like the enclosures built towards the end of the Bronze Age. Others were vast and elaborate – Maiden Castle in Dorset was one of the largest hill forts in Europe. The whole hillside was ringed with tiers of protective earthworks.

Maiden Castle hill fort in Dorset was dug in stages between about 700 and 450 BCE.

This 19th-century etching imagines a busy forge in the late Iron Age.

Some hill forts were only used as a safe refuge in time of war. Others, for example Maiden Castle, were fortified towns where people lived all the time. They were bustling communities, packed with roundhouses, barns for livestock, granaries, forges and textile workshops. The marketplace sold local produce, as well as pottery, wine, oil and glassware imported from Europe. In return, Britain was exporting tin, lead, grain, wool and animal skins.

🐾 **What tool is the blacksmith in the forge using to beat the iron into shape?**

People bartered rather than using money to buy goods. Coins like this silver one, shown at actual size, were given by rulers as gifts to friends or followers.

The Roman general Julius Caesar wrote about the use of coins in Iron Age Britain in his memoir about his campaigns in **Gaul**:

'The population is immense: homesteads, closely resembling those of the Gauls, are met with at every turn; and cattle are very numerous. Bronze or gold coins are in use, or, instead of coins, iron bars of fixed weight. Tin is found in the country in the inland, and iron in the maritime districts, but the latter only in small quantities; bronze is imported.'

WHAT WERE IRON AGE HOMES LIKE?

Most Iron Age homes were roundhouses. Their exact construction depended on the local materials available. Some had timber frames and **wattle-and-daub** walls. Others were built from stone. Roofs were thatched or covered with turf.

Inside the home, there was just one circular room. At the centre was the hearth fire. There was no chimney, but a lot of the smoke escaped naturally through the thatch. The fire heated and lit the home and was used for cooking, too. Cooking pots were made of clay, though some households had metal cauldrons that could be hung over the fire from a three-legged metal stand. Alongside the fire there was often a small clay oven for baking bread.

When women weren't cooking, grinding grain into flour or helping with the garden or livestock, they wove wool to make warm clothes for all the family. There may have been some time for relaxation, though: people drank beer, told stories, sang songs and even played board games. At night the family slept on hay mattresses, under wool blankets and animal skins.

Phil Bennett runs the Iron Age village at Castell Henllys:

'*Like any house they need regular minor repairs and maintenance, but … there is good reason to believe that well-built Iron Age roundhouses might have stood for over one hundred years.*'

🐾 **Look closely at the two roundhouses. How do we know that the one in front is a storehouse?**

These roundhouses are part of a replica Iron Age village at Castell Henllys in Pembrokeshire, Wales.

The way of life was much the same all over Britain, but there were different building styles in the far north and west. In Scotland, people built brochs – circular stone towers, up to four storeys high. These may have been lookout posts, surrounded by smaller roundhouses. Wheelhouses, also unique to Scotland, were stone buildings with spoke-like walls that divided the space into rooms. Most have been found in the Western and Northern Isles off the north coast. The largest were about 11.5 m (37.5 ft) across and housed several families.

DETECTIVE WORK

Tour the British Museum's collection to find out more about daily life during the Iron Age: www.britishmuseum. org/explore/online_tours/ britain/daily_life_in_iron_ age_britain/daily_life_in_ iron_age_britain.aspx

This wheelhouse is on Shetland, one of the Northern Isles. All its inhabitants shared the central hearth.

Crannogs were roundhouses that were constructed on artificial islands or jetties over lakes or rivers. The surrounding water made them easier to defend against raiders. So far, the remains of about 1,200 crannogs have been found in Ireland, and hundreds in Scotland.

This reconstruction of a crannog stands on Loch Tay. Around 2,600 years ago, there were 18 crannogs on the loch like this one.

WHO WERE THE CELTS?

'Celts' is the name given to lots of scattered tribes that existed across Europe during the Iron Age. The main regions of settlements were in France (the Gauls), Britain (the Britons) and Ireland and Spain and Portugal (the Celtiberians). The Britons were made up of about 30 different tribes. The Iceni, for example, inhabited eastern England.

The Celts arrived in Britain in about 600 BCE. They all spoke similar languages and shared similar customs – but they were not one big, happy family. According to Roman historians, the Celts were always warring among themselves and they wore fearsome 'war paint' – blue dye extracted from a plant called woad.

In reality, the Celts lived in tribal communities where everyone had family ties, and answered to a warrior chief or king. They were successful farmers and their craftworkers produced beautiful metalwork, pottery and jewellery. Their designs are recognizable by their strong patterns of spirals and curves. Archaeologists have unearthed many **hoards** of Celtic treasure – gold and silver coins, torcs (neck rings), bracelets, shields, daggers and swords. Some were buried in times of danger by owners who probably expected to retrieve them later. Others were offerings to the gods.

This dazzling gold torc is part of the Snettisham Hoard, which may once have belonged to an Iceni king.

Diodorus of Sicily wrote this description of the Celts:

'Some of them are clean-shaven, but others, especially those of high rank, shave their cheeks but leave a moustache that covers the whole mouth and, when they eat and drink, acts like a sieve, trapping particles of food.'

This stone head discovered in the Czech Republic dates to the 200s BCE. It shows a moustached Celt wearing a torc around his neck.

DETECTIVE WORK

Find out all about the Wetwang chariot burial here: www.britishmuseum. org/explore/online_tours/ britain/the_wetwang_ chariot_burial/the_ wetwang_chariot_burial. aspx

Although most Celts seem not to have buried their dead, hundreds of Iron Age burial sites have been found in Yorkshire. The most spectacular are the 20 or so chariot burials, where individuals were buried with their chariots. One 2,300-year-old burial at Wetwang belonged to a woman. Perhaps she was a tribal chief, a princess or a religious leader?

Bodies preserved in peat bogs are another source of information about Iron Age people. Two famous bog people are Clonycavan Man from Ireland and Lindow Man from Cheshire. Both were in their twenties, both were victims of ritual murders and both seem to have been wealthy. Lindow Man had neat nails so he could not have been a manual worker. Exactly why they were killed is a mystery, but it may have been to please the gods.

What happened to Clonycavan Man's lower body?

Clonycavan Man was discovered in a bog in County Meath, Ireland. He has traces of costly oil on his hair.

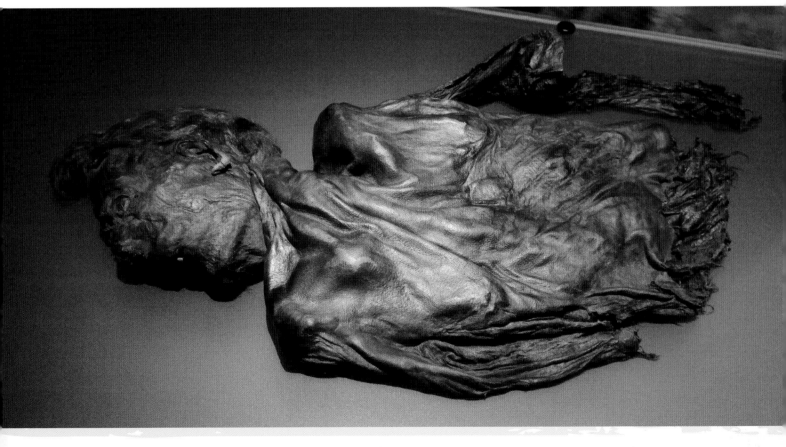

WHAT DID THE CELTS BELIEVE IN?

Just as there was no single people called the Celts, there was no single set of Celtic beliefs. However, certain practices were common among many or all tribes and certain gods crop up again and again, even if they have different names.

The Celts worshipped hundreds of gods. Some looked after an aspect of the world, such as light, dawn or thunder. Some were in charge of a particular area of human existence, for example motherhood, warfare or the afterlife. Several gods were associated with more than one idea. As farmers, the Celts were especially keen for the gods to ensure bumper harvests. They made offerings to fertility deities in the hope that they would bring times of plenty. Sucellus was a god of farming, thunder and forests, who woke up the earth each spring by striking it with his hammer. Cernunnos, an ancient god who had stag's antlers, was another provider, frequently shown feeding animals.

The horned figure on this blackened silver cauldron is Cernunnos. He looked after fertility, nature, harvests and the afterlife.

What does Epona have on her lap? They're slightly damaged, but what are the two animals on either side of her?

Epona, the goddess of horses and harvests, was worshipped long after the end of the Iron Age.

The Celts also believed in countless minor deities, who inhabited particular rocks, trees, rivers, lakes or mountains. The spirit world was everywhere! People gave gifts to these gods, throwing bronze or gold shields and helmets into rivers and burying precious torcs and other jewellery in the earth. They also tossed offerings into waterfalls, wells and springs, because they thought these places were doors from this world into the next. The Celts believed that everyone who died went to an afterlife.

Historians are not sure what sort of religious ceremonies the Celts had. They would have held feasts and ceremonies for gods on particular days of the year. Oak groves (small woods) were sacred to the Celts, and they performed special rituals there. They also worshipped in small household shrines as well as larger temples. Priests called **druids** carried out rituals to help guarantee the people's safety and prosperity. Roman writers claimed that the druids were cannibals who made human sacrifices, but they may just have wanted the Celts to seem wild and barbaric.

DETECTIVE WORK

Find out about Celtic religious beliefs here: http://celts.mrdonn.org/druids.html

This description of druids by the Roman writer Pliny the Elder was published around 79 CE:

'The druids (so they call their wise men) hold nothing in greater reverence than the mistletoe, and the tree on which it grows, so that it be an oak. They choose forests of oaks, for the sake of the tree itself, and perform no sacred rites without oak leaves … The priest clothed in a white dress [climbs] the tree, and cuts the mistletoe with a golden knife; it is caught in a white cloak. Thereupon they slay the victims, with a prayer…'

Mistletoe

This fanciful 19th-century illustration shows druids in an oak grove about to gather sacred mistletoe.

HOW DID THE IRON AGE END?

In Britain, the Iron Age ended when the Romans arrived, bringing their customs with them and changing the British landscape with their roads, towns, forts, villas and farms. Life in Britain did not change overnight, but Celtic culture slowly merged with Roman ideas and practices.

Julius Caesar was the first Roman general to invade Britain. The year was 55 BCE and he had just conquered Gaul (modern-day France and Belgium). Tribes in southern Britain drove him off, and although he returned the following year with more men, he was not able to capture the island. The Emperor Augustus planned an invasion in 34 BCE, but had to call it off because of trouble elsewhere in the empire. He also cancelled two further attacks. However, although they did not rule Britain, the Romans were still able to get their hands on its rich resources, thanks to strong trading links.

Experts believe this spectacular Iron Age shield was tossed into the River Thames as an offering to the gods. Perhaps its owner was asking for success in battle?

This statue shows the Roman general Julius Caesar, who tried but failed to conquer Iron Age Britain.

🐾 What is Caesar wearing on his head?

That all changed in the 40s CE, when the Romans worried that conflicts between warring Celts were threatening their supplies of resources such as tin and wool. In 43 CE, Emperor Claudius sent his general Aulus Plautius to subdue Britain. His forces met serious resistance in Kent, led by two princes of the Catuvellauni tribe. Eventually the Celts were defeated near Rochester and pushed back to the Thames.

Claudius celebrated his victory, but the Romans had captured only one tiny corner of Britain. There was a long way to go. Greater numbers of soldiers were sent and slowly they subdued the Celts, captured Iron Age hill forts and built their own forts to hold on to the territory they had gained. Pockets of rebellion continued for decades. Boudicca, queen of the Iceni, led a fierce campaign in 61 CE but was eventually defeated. By 84 CE the Romans had conquered as much of the country as they were going to. Most of what is now Scotland never fell and neither did Ireland, but the rest of Britain became part of the Roman Empire. The Iron Age was over.

Tacitus recorded the stirring speech Boudicca made to drum up support for her resistance movement:

'It is not as a woman descended from noble ancestry, but as one of the people that I am avenging lost freedom … a legion which dared to fight has perished; the rest are hiding themselves in their camp, or are thinking anxiously of flight. They will not sustain even the din and the shout of so many thousands, much less our charge and our blows.'

DETECTIVE WORK

Find out about Boudicca and read a poem about her: www.history-for-kids. com/boudica.html

Boudicca managed to unite several Celtic tribes in a revolt against the Romans.

YOUR PROJECT

So much happened during the period of history from the Stone Age to the Iron Age. People went from living in caves to building elaborate hill forts. They developed amazing new technologies. Think about what project you could do to make sense of it all and present some of the information you have found out.

You might choose to produce a timeline. You could start about 800,000 years ago when people arrived in Britain, and end with the coming of the Romans. The choice of entries is up to you. Your timeline could cover the whole British Isles or just your area. Do you have a local museum? See what prehistoric objects are in its collection. Do not forget to spend time out and about in the landscape, too. There might be ancient burial mounds, standing stones or other monuments near you, or perhaps a reconstructed village. Sketch or photograph what you see so that you can add pictures to your timeline.

You might prefer to take inspiration from one period to produce some amazing art. You could make your own 'Ice Age' engravings by scratching animal outlines onto old pieces of bone or wood – find out what wild animals lived in Britain during the Stone Age. Or try your hand at a 'prehistoric' cave painting of an animal hunt. If you like graphic design, look for books of Celtic patterns and start a collection of them.

There are prehistoric remains all over Britain. This is part of the Broch of Gurness, an Iron Age settlement on Orkney.

You might have your own ideas for a project, but whatever you decide, remember it is your project, so choose something that interests you. Good luck!

Project presentation

- Do plenty of research before you begin. Use the Internet and your local or school library. Is there a nearby museum, historical site or society related to your project? Many of these will also have their own Internet site.

- Experiment with different styles of writing. You could write up your timeline entries as straightforward factual sentences. Or you could choose to write them as if they were diary entries or blog posts. It's up to you.

- Collect pictures to illustrate your project. Print off images from the Internet. Buy postcards in museums. Take photographs or make your own sketches whenever you visit an important site.

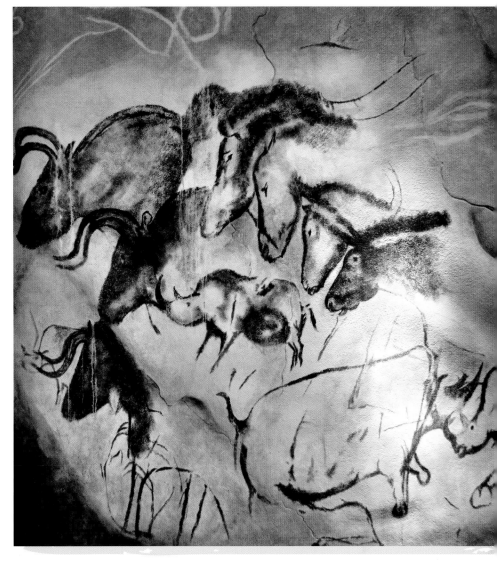

Find examples of cave art in books or online. This painting is one of hundreds in Chauvet Cave, south-central France, that date back 30,000 years.

This swimming reindeer was carved onto a mammoth tusk around 11,000 BCE.

GLOSSARY

archaeologist Someone who studies the remains of past societies.

barrow A large mound, often built to mark a burial site.

barter To trade by swapping goods, not using money.

BCE 'Before the Common Era'. Used to signify years before the believed birth of Jesus, around 2,000 years ago.

Beaker A culture and people in western Europe during the early Bronze Age.

Bronze Age The period when people learned to work metal. In Britain, it lasted from around 2500 to 800 BCE.

CE 'Common Era'. Used to signify years since the believed birth of Jesus.

dolmen A Neolithic monument, where a flat stone rests on some upright stones, often built to mark a grave.

druid A Celtic priest.

evolution The process by which living things change over long periods of time and may give rise to new species.

flint A very hard stone.

Gaul The Roman name for France and Belgium, or one of the region's people.

grave goods Objects placed in tombs for use in the afterlife.

hand axe A flint cutting tool that fits in the hand.

henge A circular ditch and bank of earth built as a monument, sometimes topped with standing stones or wooden pillars.

hill fort A hilltop fortified by defensive ditches and banks.

hoard Buried treasure.

hunter-gatherer Someone who lives by hunting, fishing and collecting wild foods.

ice age A period when the climate is so cold that ice sheets cover the ground.

Iron Age The period of history when people learned to work iron. In Britain, it lasted from around 800 BCE until the Romans arrived in 43 CE. In Ireland, it lasted until around 400 CE.

Mesolithic Age The Middle Stone Age. The period when people were hunter-gatherers using advanced stone tools. In Britain, it lasted from around 9500 to 4000 BCE.

Neolithic Age The New Stone Age. The period when people began to farm. In Britain, it lasted from around 4000 to 2500 BCE.

Paleolithic Age The Old Stone Age. The period when people used simple tools of stone, wood and bone. In Britain, it lasted from around 800,000 to 11,500 years ago.

prehistoric The time before written records. In Britain, prehistory ended with the arrival of the Romans in 43 CE.

shaman A tribesperson in contact with the spirit world.

solstice Midsummer or midwinter. In Britain, which is in the northern half of the world, these fall on 21 June and 22 December.

wattle-and-daub Built of posts and twigs (wattle) and clay or mud and straw (daub).

ANSWERS

Page 5:   The harpoons were carved from bone.

Page 7:   They hunted many different animals, including deer, elk, wild boar, bears and beavers.

Page 9:   They wrapped them in animal skins, so the flint was not chipped as it was carried to the surface.

Page 11:   Spirals and diamonds decorate the entrance stone to Newgrange.

Page 13:   The sarsen horseshoe was made up of five trilithons (a trilithon is a grouping of three stones – two uprights and one lintel). Five groups of three stones makes 15 stones in total.

Page 15:   The wooden handle is a reconstruction – the original rotted away long ago. This flesh hook was discovered in Little Thetford in Cambridgeshire in 1929.

Page 16:   They buried their dead with grave goods – belongings that they would need in the afterlife.

Page 19:   He is using a hammer to beat the metal into shape.

Page 21:   The front roundhouse is raised on stilts to help prevent rats from raiding the stores.

Page 23:   His lower body was probably chopped off by peat-cutting machinery. Bog people are usually found in peat bogs by workers who are harvesting peat, an important fuel.

Page 24:   She has a basket of fruit on her lap, symbolizing fertility, and horses on either side of her.

Page 26:   Caesar wears a laurel wreath (crown of laurel leaves) as a symbol of his military successes.

FURTHER INFORMATION

Books to read
The Celts (The History Detective Investigates) by Philip Steele (Wayland, 2011)
Early People (Eyewitness) (Dorling Kindersley, 2003)
Prehistoric Britain by Alex Firth (Usborne, 2010)
The Secrets of Stonehenge by Mick Manning and Brita Granström (Frances Lincoln, 2013)

Websites
www.stonepages.com
www.bbc.co.uk/wales/celts/
www.mustfarm.com
Note to parents and teachers: Every effort has been made by the publishers to ensure that these websites are suitable for children. However, because of the nature of the Internet, it is impossible to guarantee that the contents of these sites will not be altered. We strongly advise that Internet access is supervised by a responsible adult.

Places to visit
British Museum, London WC1B 3DG
Creswell Crags, near Worksop S80 3LH
Flag Fen, Peterborough PE6 7QJ
Stonehenge, near Salisbury SP4 7DE